W9-CAR-452

Afraid of the Water

Box Jellyfish
Killer Tentacles

by Natalie Lunis

Consultant: Jamie Seymour, Associate Professor
School of Marine and Tropical Biology
James Cook University

BEARPORT
PUBLISHING

New York, New York

Credits

Cover and Title Page, © Paul Sutherland/National Geographic/Getty Images; 4, © Chris McLennan/Alamy; 5, © David Doubilet/National Geographic Stock; 6, © imagebroker / Alamy; 7, © Newspix; 8, © Gary Bell/OceanwideImages.com; 9, © Curtis Kautzer/Shutterstock; 10, © Roger Steene/Image Quest Marine; 11, © Anders Garm; 12, © Auscape/ardea.com; 13, © Ross Armstrong/SeaPics.com; 14,.© Peter Arnold, Inc./Alamy; 15, © Paul Sutherland/NGS Image Collection; 17, © Paul Sutherland/NGS Image Collection; 18, © David Wall/Alamy; 19, © Les Bazo/Province; 20, © Dr. David Wachenfeld/Auscape/Minden Pictures; 21, © imagebroker/Alamy; 22T, © Scott Leslie; 22B, © AFP Photo/Lisa-Ann Gerswhin; 24, © Roger Steene/Image Quest Marine.

Publisher: Kenn Goin
Editorial Director: Adam Siegel
Creative Director: Spencer Brinker
Photo Researcher: Picture Perfect Professionals, LLC
Design: Dawn Beard Creative

Library of Congress Cataloging-in-Publication Data

Lunis, Natalie.
  Box jellyfish : killer tentacles / by Natalie Lunis.
    p. cm. — (Afraid of the water)
  Includes bibliographical references and index.
  ISBN-13: 978-1-59716-945-5 (library binding)
  ISBN-10: 1-59716-945-5 (library binding)
  1. Cubomedusae—Juvenile literature. I. Title.

  QL377.S4L857 2010
  593.5'3—dc22

                          2009007603

For more information, write to Bearport Publishing Company, Inc., 101 Fifth Avenue, Suite 6R, New York, New York 10003. Printed in the United States of America in North Mankato, Minnesota.

112009
102309CG

10 9 8 7 6 5 4 3 2

Contents

Stung!

Jade Hudson-Clark was having fun at the beach. The 11-year-old girl had gone for a swim in the warm waters of the Pacific Ocean near Townsville, Australia. Her two friends, Chelsea, 13, and Erin, 15, were splashing around nearby.

Then something went wrong. Jade felt as though a hundred pins were going into her leg. Chelsea and Erin heard Jade call out that she couldn't swim. They hurried over and pulled her out of the water. Their friend was not out of danger, however. The girls didn't know for certain yet, but Jade had been stung by a box jellyfish—the deadliest, most **venomous** sea creature in the world.

Townsville, Australia

DANGER

In Australia, box jellyfish are also known as "boxies" and "stingers."

A box jellyfish swimming in the ocean near Townsville, Australia

Beach Rescue

When Jade was stung, she felt something stringy wrap around her leg. She tried kicking it off, but that didn't work. Neither did trying to swim away. A horrible, needle-like pain slowed her down. She also felt her heart start to beat very fast. That's why she called out for help.

After Jade's friends pulled her out of the water, they took more steps to save her life. Chelsea ran to a lifeguard station and came back with a bottle of vinegar. She poured it over the stings on Jade's body. Then she waved down a passing car. The driver called for an ambulance, which took Jade to a nearby hospital. After spending a night there, Jade was allowed to go home. She was soon back to normal, except for some scars from the sting.

VINEGAR
FOR USE ON MARINE STINGS
POUR ON - DO NOT RUB
*SEEK MEDICAL ATTENTION

DANGER

Vinegar is kept at lifeguard stations in northern Australia, where Townsville is located, in case jellyfish stings need to be treated.

In this photo, Jade (center) gets a hug from her friends Erin (left) and Chelsea (right).

A Different Kind of Jellyfish

In most ways, box jellyfish are like other kinds of jellyfish. For example, a box jellyfish's boneless body is made up of a jelly-filled top called a **bell**, which has long, stringy **tentacles** hanging down. The tentacles contain many tiny stingers that can send **venom** into the bodies of other animals.

There are important differences, however, between box jellyfish and regular, or "true," jellyfish. The difference that is easiest to see is in the shape of the bell. A true jellyfish's bell is rounded. Often it is shaped like a bowl. A box jellyfish's bell has sides and rounded corners—it is shaped like a box.

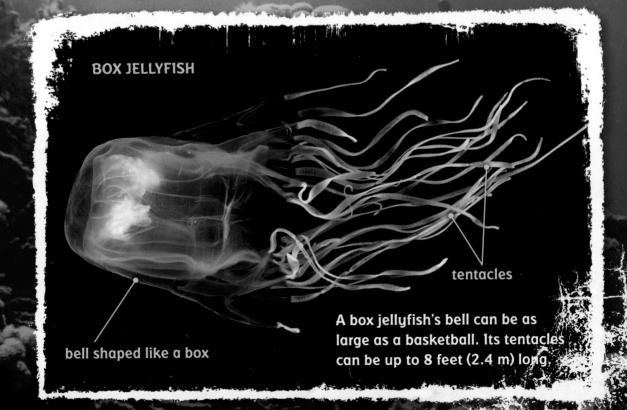

BOX JELLYFISH

tentacles

bell shaped like a box

A box jellyfish's bell can be as large as a basketball. Its tentacles can be up to 8 feet (2.4 m) long.

bell shaped
like a bowl

tentacles

DANGER

Scientists place true jellyfish
and box jellyfish into two
different groups. True
jellyfish are *scyphozoans*
(*sye*-fuh-ZOH-uhnz)—
meaning "bowl animals."
Box jellyfish are *cubozoans*
(*kyoob*-uh-ZOH-uhnz)—
meaning "cube animals."

9

24 Eyes, 4 Brains

A box jellyfish has a different shape than a true jellyfish. It also has something that no true jellyfish has—eyes. In fact, the deadly creature has 24 of them.

The box jellyfish's 24 eyes are grouped in four clusters. Each cluster has six eyes and is on a different side of the bell. Four of the eyes in each group are fairly simple. They can only tell light from dark. The other two are more complex. Scientists think that they allow the box jellyfish to see the color and size of objects. With so many eyes, it's not too surprising that the box jellyfish has more than one brain. In fact, it has four brains to help it make sense of what it sees.

DANGER

The eyes on a box jellyfish help keep it from bumping into objects as it swims in the ocean.

eye cluster

Swimming and Stinging

Both true jellyfish and box jellyfish use their stinging tentacles to catch shrimp and small fish for food. However, box jellyfish are more active hunters than true jellyfish. After all, they can see their **prey**. They are also better swimmers.

A true jellyfish swims by opening and closing its bell. Each time the bell closes, water shoots out, and the jellyfish moves. However, a true jellyfish moves very slowly and swims only to get to places where food is likely to float by. It does not chase after its prey. A box jellyfish, on the other hand, can swim much faster. It uses its speed—and its eyesight—to chase down the small animals that it stings and eats.

Like true jellyfish, box jellyfish swim by opening and closing their bells. However, they swim much faster than true jellyfish.

DANGER
A box jellyfish can swim at speeds of up to four miles per hour (6.4 kph)—that's faster than many people can swim.

True jellyfish like the one above float in the sea, waiting for their next meal to get caught in their stinging tentacles.

Deadly Venom

Coiled up inside a box jellyfish's tentacles are thousands of tiny stingers. Each stinger is filled with deadly venom. When a tentacle brushes against a shrimp or a small fish, the stingers uncoil and shoot the venom into the prey's body. The tentacles then pull the victim up to the bottom of the jellyfish's bell—where the creature's mouth is. Because the prey has been stunned or quickly killed by the venom, it does not fight or struggle.

box jellyfish tentacles

A box jellyfish has up to 60 tentacles — with up to 15 of them hanging from each corner of its bell.

DANGER

The uncoiling of a jellyfish's tiny stingers is one of the fastest actions in nature. Scientists have found that the stingers shoot out even faster than a bullet from a gun.

A box jellyfish's deadly venom keeps its victim from struggling and escaping.

fish

A Danger to People?

The venom from a box jellyfish can kill a person. Yet these deadly sea creatures don't chase swimmers, and they don't try to sting them. In fact, they try to avoid humans and other large animals. So how do people get stung?

Most stings occur when people bump into box jellyfish tentacles while swimming or accidentally step on them in shallow water. A box jellyfish's clear body and long tentacles make it almost invisible in the ocean. Swimmers and beachgoers almost never see it before they are stung.

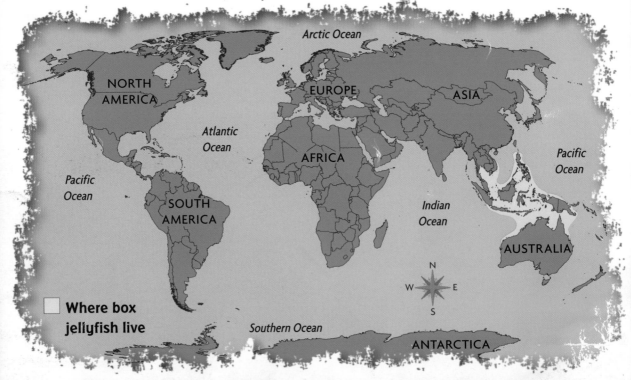

Box Jellyfish in the Wild

Arctic Ocean

NORTH AMERICA

EUROPE

ASIA

Atlantic Ocean

AFRICA

Pacific Ocean

Pacific Ocean

SOUTH AMERICA

Indian Ocean

AUSTRALIA

Southern Ocean

ANTARCTICA

Where box jellyfish live

Box jellyfish live in the ocean waters off northern Australia and parts of Southeast Asia.

This man fishes dangerously close to a box jellyfish.

DANGER

On average, one person per year is killed in Australia by a box jellyfish's sting. Experts think that the deadly creature may kill as many as 100 people per year in other parts of the world, such as Indonesia, Thailand, and the Philippines.

Treating Stings

Lifeguards and other rescuers have to act fast after a box jellyfish stings a swimmer. A bad sting can kill a person by stopping his or her heart in about two minutes.

Once a victim is out of the water, the rescuer needs to decide how bad the injury is. If the victim's heart has stopped, the rescuer should perform **CPR**. Then vinegar should be poured over the sting. Why? Pieces of stinging tentacles are often left on the victim's skin. If there are any stingers that have not fired yet, the vinegar stops them from firing and releasing more venom. In serious cases, victims also need to be rushed to a hospital.

DANGER

Scientists have developed an **antivenom** for box jellyfish stings. In the parts of Australia where box jellyfish are a problem, ambulances and hospitals keep this life-saving drug on hand.

If treated in time, people can survive box jellyfish stings. However, the stings usually leave bad scars.

Staying Safe

Vinegar and antivenom can help swimmers after they have been stung by box jellyfish. However, people are also working on ways to prevent swimmers from getting stung in the first place.

Many beaches put up warning signs if there is any chance that box jellyfish are in the water. Some beaches also have **stinger nets** set up to keep the jellyfish from coming too close to swimmers. Steps like these are helping to bring down the number of deaths caused by box jellyfish. The strange cube-shaped creatures are still out there, but people are learning to stay away from their deadly stingers.

A box jellyfish swimming near the surface of the ocean in Cleveland Bay, Queensland, Australia

DANGER

To protect their bodies from jellyfish stings, some swimmers and lifeguards wear stinger suits—bathing suits that cover almost every part of the body.

Beaches in Australia put up warning signs if there are box jellyfish or other dangerous stinging creatures in the water.

MARINE STINGERS ARE PRESENT IN THESE WATERS DURING THE SUMMER MONTHS

Other Stinging Jellyfish

The box jellyfish is the most venomous of all jellyfish. In fact, it is the most venomous of all sea creatures. Other jellyfish also have dangerous, though less deadly, stings.

Lion's Mane Jellyfish

- One of the largest of the true jellyfish, it has tentacles up to 120 feet (36.6 m) in length. Its bell can measure up to 7 feet, 6 inches (2.3 m) across.
- It lives in oceans around the world.
- In spite of its huge size, it feeds on small fish, shrimp, and small jellyfish.
- Its sting is painful but not deadly for a person.

Irukandji (ee-roo-KAHN-jee)

- Like the box jellyfish, this box-shaped creature is a cubozoan rather than a true jellyfish. It is found in warm waters around the world.
- Unlike the box jellyfish, it is tiny, with a bell that is about the size of a peanut.
- Because of its small size, it is sometimes able to slip through stinger nets designed to keep box jellyfish away from swimmers at beaches.
- Its sting is very dangerous and can cause terrible pain, muscle cramps, and vomiting.

Glossary

antivenom (*an*-tee-VEN-uhm) a medicine that blocks the effects of venom

bell (BELL) the clear top part of a jellyfish's body

CPR (SEE-PEE-AR) letters standing for *cardiopulmonary resuscitation*—a type of rescue where a person blows air into the mouth and then presses down on the chest of someone whose heart has stopped

prey (PRAY) animals that are hunted by other animals for food

stinger nets (STING-ur NETS) nets put up to create safe swimming areas at beaches by keeping jellyfish out

tentacles (TEN-tuh-kuhlz) stinging body parts that hang down from a jellyfish's bell

venom (VEN-uhm) poison that some animals can send into the bodies of other animals through a bite or sting

venomous (VEN-uhm-uhss) able to attack with a poisonous bite or sting

Index

Bibliography

Johnson, Leonie. "Mates Saved My Life." *Townsville Bulletin* (January 15, 2008).

Parker, Steve. *Sponges, Jellyfish, and Other Simple Animals.* Minneapolis, MN: Compass Point Books (2006).

www.abc.net.au/catalyst/stories/s1073805.htm

Read More

Brennan, Joseph K. *Jellyfish and Other Stingers.* Chicago: World Book, Inc. (2006).

Earle, Sylvia A. *Sea Critters.* Washington, D.C.: National Geographic Society (2000).

McFee, Shane. *Jellyfish.* New York: Rosen (2008).

Learn More Online

To learn more about the box jellyfish, visit
www.bearportpublishing.com/AfraidoftheWater

About the Author

Natalie Lunis has written many science and nature books for children. She lives in the Hudson River Valley, just north of New York City.